The **Nalleslavski Method** is the s
lowest common denominator of laughter. The Nalleslavski
pedagogy has been focused on helping performers create
characters and material so they can perform a show of
their own creation, anywhere in the world.

The Clown's Ten Commandments

1. Enjoy the game

2. Connect with your audience

3. Comfort the disturbed. Disturb the comfortable.

4. Don't try to be funny, be real.

5. Have a bag of tricks

6. If it works, do it again, more.

7. If it doesn't work, try something else.

8. Start under your audience's energy level
    and bring them up with you to a climax.

9. Dare to really fail

10. Dare to really succeed

11. Accept presents from the clown gods

THE
CLOWN
MANIFESTO

THE CLOWN MANIFESTO

P. Nalle Laanela
&
Stacey Sacks

Based on P. Nalle Laanela's
international research on physical comedy

First published in 2015 by Oberon Books Ltd
521 Caledonian Road, London N7 9RH
Tel: +44 (0) 20 7607 3637 / Fax: +44 (0) 20 7607 3629
e-mail: info@oberonbooks.com
www.oberonbooks.com

A catalogue record for this book is available from the British Library.

PB ISBN: 978-1-78319-119-2
E ISBN: 978-1-78319-618-0

Cover illustration by Mathias Broberg / Mani

Printed, bound and converted
by CPI Group (UK) Ltd, Croydon, CR0 4YY.

Visit www.oberonbooks.com to read more about all our books and to buy them. You will also find features, author interviews and news of any author events, and you can sign up for e-newsletters so that you're always first to hear about our new releases.

The not so silly art of the physical comedian
according to *Nalleslavski**

* *Nalleslavski* is a method created by P. Nalle Laanela through
which performers can develop more connected
and playful relationships with their audiences.

List of Contents

If performance art disconnects from the community it's performing for, it dies.

The more trauma one has experienced, the bigger the need to laugh.

*It's not about acting stupid,
it's about daring to be perceived as stupid.*

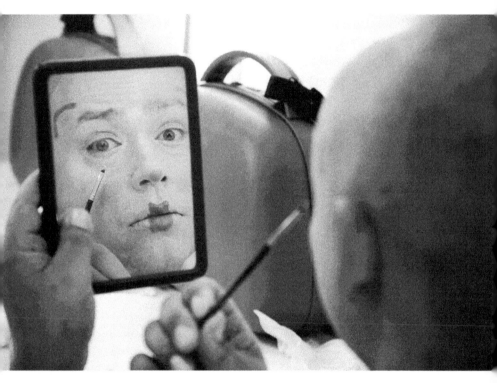

Photograph © Lotta Andersson

About the Author

P. Nalle Laanela lives in a blue bus. He started his career as a failed actor, then became an overweight dancer, until he finally found his calling as a clown. He studied physical comedy at the Dell'Arte School of Physical Comedy in California, at L'École Internationale de Théâtre Jacques Lecoq in Paris as well as with several of the clown teacher greats, but most of what he has learned he was taught by the eclectic audiences he has met around the world. When he founded the arts NGO Clowns Without Borders – Sweden, in 1996, he started his lifetime research into defining the universal lowest common denominator of laughter.

Nalle's work as a clown and show director is focused through his company Circus Arts and its internationally touring productions *Moulin Noir* and *The Burnt Out Punks*.

As Associate Professor of Clown, his passion for pedagogy led him to work with performers at the Stockholm Academy of Dance and Circus and at the Stockholm Academy of Dramatic Arts where he was Clown Professor for a Master's programme entitled 'A Year of Physical Comedy'.

Nalle's teaching and directing experiences guided him towards the dream of sharing some of his tools and thoughts in written form, and entitling them 'The Nalleslavski Method'. Your hands now hold that dream.

'Happiness is most important.'
Nalleslavski

*Inside
Nalle's
blue bus*

Photograph © Evy Maroon

Foreword

by Stacey Sacks

I was daunted when Nalle first asked me to help collate his ideas in the form of a book. On a Clowns Without Borders – Sweden expedition to Rwanda in 2011 I tried to make children participate in a call and response game, and failed miserably. There's nothing quite like being a clown and having thousands of children stare blankly at you as if you are a complete idiot, and not in the good sense. With hindsight I realise it was because I didn't truly understand what my clown professor, Nalle, was trying to teach me at the time, as part of a Master's course entitled 'A Year of Physical Comedy' at the Stockholm Academy of Dramatic Arts. In that moment I was too consumed by my own performance, too self-conscious, worrying about my character and so-called 'truth' and not focusing on the audience's experience there and then.

Coming from an acting background, I was trained mostly in the teachings of Constantin Stanislavski and Jerzy Grotowski, both of whom (to be ridiculously simple) have performance philosophies which place the performer strongly in the centre of the creative process. It is here that Nalle's concept of performance strays from the traditional pedagogic path. *Nalleslavski* holds the audience as supreme. The performer exists because of them, it is the audience's emotional journey which is paramount and around which the entire performance must revolve.

I've watched Nalle live out his clown philosophy. On Clowns Without Borders expeditions to Rwanda, Myanmar and Jordan, I witnessed and experienced *Nalleslavski* in motion. On dusty roads in Gisenyi, near the border with

Congo, adults and children giggled, laughed and stared in awe and amazement as Nalle pulled out trick after trick, lifting his audience out of their ordinary realities, transforming people's worlds in that brief and beautiful moment. At 2 a.m. one morning at a bizarre truck stop on a remote Burmese highway between Yangon and Mandalay, I remember young girls selling small boiled speckly eggs, stopping by our car and watching Nalle do magic. I see their exuberant faces still, the look of wonder and delight in their eyes was unforgettable. It is because of these experiences that I know *Nalleslavski* works as a method for finding a connection and creating a sense of playfulness with one's audience.

The eggs tasted terrible, by the way.

Not only have I seen Nalle performing his clown philosophy on the streets of Rwanda, Myanmar and in a Syrian refugee camp on the border with Jordan, but also on the alternative burlesque stages of Stockholm's underground queer scene, and as *Inferno* in his fire circus BURNT OUT PUNKS. Whether he's playing his Clowns Without Borders character *Nalle Blue*, or singing provocatively as *Coco Belle* in his black corset and giant pink eyelashes, he's always using elements of *Nalleslavski*.

During my year of study in Stockholm, I created a solo show, *I Shit Diamonds*, for which Nalle was an 'outside eye'. It's an adult clown comedy about dictatorship, and was a large portion of my artistic research, investigating the elastic relationship between the actor and clown and the physical language of power through parody and satire. During the process of creating the show, after several public performances, I arrived at a concept of the performer-clown being 'on' the moment, which we've included in the 'Improvisation and Gifts From the Clown Gods' section.

In documentary film-making and journalism, there's a concept called pulsation. It's the moving back and forth from the subject to yourself, all the way. Clowning is like this, a constant pulsation between the clown and audience – a living, breathing organism. Of course, I like to think it's a spiritual enactment, a communion between humans, affirming our common humanity. But sometimes, as happened to me recently at a children's birthday party gig, it's just being attacked by sugar-infested cretins who repeatedly pull your pants down, steal your props, kick you, stick their fatty sugar fingers on your boobs to check whether you're a girl or boy and a bunch of other stuff that'll have you crying at the bus stop on your way home and being comforted by kind strangers.

Whatever form your clowning takes, Nalle's method gives you graspable tools to create comedy material that works universally, across cultural and language barriers. But before you get too comfortable and think you're doing a good deed by making people laugh, his good-natured phrase 'Happiness is most important' juxtaposes his perception that 'just because the audience is laughing, doesn't mean they like you or what you are doing'. *Nalleslavski* bites.

His method goes deeply into the relationship between the audience and the performer and, as I've learned, it's never as straightforward as the creator or the audience tend to imagine. It's a tightrope made of spaghetti, there are no guarantees, but there are definitely techniques. Implementing the tools suggested by Nalle in this book will ensure a constantly improving performance, and the analytical skills to break a solo show up into its constituent parts in order to build the comedy.

At the beginning of the writing process, I was fearful of misrepresenting Nalle's method but, thankfully, the final product has emerged out of many conversations between us. After endless Skype dates between Johannesburg and Stockholm, months of fragmented discussions in city coffee shops, convoluted analysis about the art of the comedic physical performer, as well as several powwows on his island in the Swedish Archipelago, we can finally offer you *The Clown Manifesto*.

Stacey Sacks, Stockholm, June 2014

Prologue

People believe either you're funny or you're not. Not only do I not believe this, but I've spent my life and career trying to figure out the mechanisms of the comedic performer's craft and how audiences react. Humour can be trained, even if talent is a bonus. Everyone has the ability to be creative and funny, it's about understanding the tricks of the trade as well as a good dose of time, commitment, possibilities and getting out of your own way. It also helps if you find yourself in a social context which both nurtures and encourages these factors.

I became a clown after trying to be serious about being a dancer. Starting my career in Vancouver as a dancer, there were a multitude of long-legged professional ballerinas, myself and lots of simultaneous choreography. Every time I arrived on stage, the audience laughed. The more I tried to be a dancer, the more they laughed. This was terrible for me. One day after an intentionally non-funny dance performance where everyone laughed again, I was approached by a small Italian clown teacher who told me I was a funny clown and invited me to do a workshop with her. She totally offended me, it went against all the ideals I was striving for. So I tried even more seriously to be a dancer, which made the audience laugh harder. I became angry, went to the clown workshop anyway and then felt like a nun must feel when she decides to follow the calling. Like a golden arc coming through the clouds, I found my clown calling. Unfortunately I then spent the next few years trying to be a small Italian female clown. What seemed to work so brilliantly for her was disastrous for me as a large white male. Many things did work though and this started my career in researching laughter's lowest common denominator. By performing internationally in multiple spaces and in front of infinitely different people, I've tried to develop material that works equally well for a corporate dinner show in Sweden and a refugee camp in Nepal.

It's strange because inherently I don't feel like a funny person, yet somehow I've managed to make a living out of humour and comedy. I've based my entire career on it. While some performers might get hired specifically because they're funny, I think I'm hired because people find me warm, generous and openly communicative with my audience. But that's not enough. I want to learn how to create mayhem and hysteria in an audience, how to take them to that edge of chaos which allows them to release their emotions cathartically. As a performer, director and teacher, I'm interested in discovering the tools for creating conditions for the audience in which they can lose control of their emotions.

Children play by acting out their imaginations, they release their emotions all the time, without screening or doubt. When children are sad, they cry. If they're angry, they scream and fall to the ground in tantrums. As we become adults we are taught to control our emotions. Extreme emotions become taboo, they get locked inside of us and we can never get over it. We are taught it is not adult-like behaviour to cry on the bus, to be afraid of the dark or laugh at the shape of vegetables at the grocery store. Yet it is my belief that, like the child's, the adult body has the same need to emotionally cleanse and the purpose of my art is to try to take the audience to that place.

Art is a justified and socially condoned reason for people to lose control of their emotions. It's ok to cry at a movie, laugh at a play and scream at a concert. I believe that part of the performer's role in society is to help people stay healthy and balanced by giving them opportunities to experience emotional catharsis. This has always been the main drive in the art I've created. Of course, I can't say that the art I've created has actually managed to affect anybody, but that doesn't stop me from trying.

This book tries to figure out what the lowest common denominator for audience laughter is, and to explain the tools so that anyone performing can use them.

I'm also sharing some thoughts and ramblings based on my experiences as a performer, creator, teacher and director in the different fields of clowning, street theatre, burlesque and so on. 'Performer' for me is a better word than 'artist', it's clearer and doesn't have any of the expectations and preconceptions of the elusive 'artist' archetype. In this book I use it interchangeably to refer to anyone who works in front of an audience: clowns, physical comedians, musicians, jugglers, puppeteers, magicians, street performers, dancers and actors too. In fact, anyone who wants to develop a sense of connection and playfulness with their audience.

What we all have in common is that we are wonder-makers.

II

History of the Wondermakers

'If performance art disconnects
from the community it's performing for,
it dies.'

Nalleslavski

Historically I feel connected to all the people who for
whatever reason have found a way to create wonder in
an audience. Whether it be the magic-using Egyptian
priests, the cup and ball scoundrel of the Medieval
streets or contemporary circus performers. We are all
wonder-makers.

As a performer I feel connected to the storytelling
grandmother, the magical shaman and the travelling
market-place performers. In all three cases the
connection between the performer and the audience

is very clear and tangible. These days, when I see performances that lack this connection I often feel they have misunderstood their true history and role in society. It sounds judgmental. And it probably is.

I call what I do Popular Theatre, it's for people. The method I use is loosely based on nothing in particular, it's called the *Nalleslavski Method*. This can be applied to storytelling, clowning, magic, circus, commedia dell'arte, street dance and any form where the performer directly communicates with their audience. In other words, everything outside of the fourth wall. The Nalleslavski Method could also be applied to classical theatre, ballet and opera productions should they choose to try it out (terms and conditions apply).

My art form is not about political buzzwords or fulfilling financiers' agendas, it's about performing in front of audiences. In my eyes it doesn't matter if you do magic or ballet, your primary art isn't being a magician or ballet dancer, your primary art is to connect with your audience. The rest is a matter of artistic preference.

Today, trying to connect with the audience is fundamentally a rebellious action since traditional systems don't seem to find the audience important. Actors are taught to zone into their inner world, jugglers are focused on their objects and dancers generally look into middle distance, not making direct eye contact with their audiences. Within the pedagogical institution of the performance arts, teachers are focusing on teaching the technique of the handstand and not the technique of making the wonder. The person who can write a thesis about the handstand now has more power than the person who can do the handstand. In my eyes, the practical wonder-making craft is being diminished and the audience's reaction ignored. If performance art forms connected with audiences already then *Nalleslavski* wouldn't have to exist, it's the void that my tools are trying to fill. My dream is to create tools that all performers can use to enhance their connection to their audiences.

Confessions of a War Clown

'The more trauma one has experienced,
the bigger the need to laugh.'

Nalleslavski

A story from Sarajevo

In the beginning of my clowning career a lot of the
important ideas and philosophies in the field seemed
to have derived from Jacques Lecoq, so I decided
to attend his school in Paris. Just as interesting as
Lecoq's theories was meeting and playing with like-
minded performers from all over the world. There I
met a quirky English magician, Bertie. We would sit
up all night drinking red wine and practising the arts
of magic, ventriloquism and pick-pocketing.

We developed a duo show which on the weekends we performed outside the Pompidou Centre, mixing magic tricks with slapstick routines. We never were very successful at making money, but it ignited my love for performing in the street. So, when the Easter holiday arrived in 1996 and I had two weeks with nothing to do, the idea to travel to Sarajevo to do street shows emerged. Peace had just arrived with Carl Bildt's peace talks and the Dayton Agreement. I took the train to Croatia but had to switch to a bus for the last section of the journey as the railway tracks were destroyed from the bombings. The bus trip was bizarre, the scenery a mixture of ex-Yugoslavia's amazing and varied landscape combined with blasted houses and villages.

We arrived in Sarajevo via a great highway, lined with stately high-rise office buildings, riddled with holes like Swiss cheese, surrounded by barbed wire and UN military vehicles. The first problem came up when I went to buy a city map. My US dollars were totally useless, the man at the kiosk just shook his head. I had exchanged my entire travel funds into US dollars, but soon realised only Deutschmarks were accepted. Hungry and anxious, I walked into town, hoping to find a bank or currency exchange bureau. It seems these always exist, even at wartime. I found three banks, but all were closed for the weekend. Famished by now, and with a slightly growing concern, I was advised by a passerby to ask the American Embassy if I could exchange the money there.

When I finally found the embassy at the edge of town, easily recognisable by the ugly architecture, extremely militarised security zone around it and the winding queue of people in front of it, I was rebuffed by the soldier guards. Go find a bank!

Dejected, I sat on the grass across the road and felt the concern was not so small anymore. The sun was going down and, as the air gradually became colder, I felt terribly alone in the world. From the corner of my eye I saw a passing jeep with a 'Doctors Without Borders' logo on it. For some reason I started running after the car. Luckily, it turned off the main road into smaller streets which made it possible for me to almost catch up with it. But with my big backpack and my suitcase full of juggling props, magic tricks and clown costume, I lost sight of the car after about ten blocks. Fortunately, I soon found it again, parked outside the 'Doctors Without Borders' offices. I ran up the stairs into the building and when I breathlessly told my whole story to the woman behind the desk, she cheerfully replied, 'A clown! Oh what fun! I know exactly who needs you.'

A phone call later I had an address and a street map from her and from there I went to the youngest NGO I have ever encountered: 'Phoenix'.

'Phoenix' consisted of a group of 16-year-old girls who for years had provided the little bit of aid that had managed to get through the Serbs' encirclement for the schools, kindergartens and children who needed it.

In war, you grow old quickly. My estimate is that experiencing one war year is equivalent to three ordinary years. A ten-year-old who has survived three years of war thus has the emotional maturity of about a nineteen-year-old.

Three years before, when these thirteen-year-old girls noticed how the international NGO's lack of local knowledge meant that assistance wavered, they took matters into their own hands and created 'Phoenix', an organisation which served as a main link between international NGOs and Sarajevo's children.

In the last year of the war, one of the girls had managed to smuggle herself out of the country and now went to college in the United States. I stayed in her room, her parents became mine and this became my virgin tour as a war clown.

During one of my first shows in Sarajevo in the old neighbourhood, my show was hijacked by a bunch of Spaniards. I had to let them join in because they were funnier than I was. After the show, they said they called themselves 'Payasos Sin Fronteras', Clowns Without Borders.

The penny dropped: I love travelling, I love meeting people and I love to perform. What a great idea. So when I returned to Sweden I gathered some artist friends and we formed Clowns Without Borders – Sweden. We started our first office in the mail room at the theatre in which I was working, and all these years later we're still here (different premises though), working with the largest international aid organisations focused on culture-based psycho-social rehabilitation projects.

A story from the West Sahara

Her sari caught fire from the gas stove on the floor of the kitchen, causing the room to explode.

The temperature in the emergency room is 45 degrees Celsius and it's so dark that the only thing I can see is two piles of blankets.

Under one is the mother who is dying.

Under the other is the boy who might survive.

The only sound in the room is their tormented breath.

I stand leaning over the boy and try to meet his eyes between the yellow bandages and the flakes of burned skin.

I show him a small red cloth in my hand and with a small magical movement, it disappears.

I see his eyes widen, searching the room.

Reaching gently towards him, I find the red cloth behind his ear.

Behind the bandages, I see a smile light up his face.

One of the most difficult expeditions I've ever been on was to schools and hospitals in the Western Saharan refugee camps situated in the deserts of Algeria, the area that God forgot.

It's so hot there that moving is impossible during the midday hours. When the water trucks break down in the desert there is nothing to drink that day. The hospitals are in a worse condition than the people they're looking after. The level of trauma is unimaginable. And yet, in this totally non-human-friendly environment, I feel a glimpse of the sense of humanity generated by our art.

Performing for the burnt child in the West Saharan refugee camp was one of the most important moments of my career so far. Evoking that smile from him was the best gift. I'll remember that smile more as a trophy of success than a hundred thousand people I've met and forgotten since.

A story from Nepal

In our Clowns Without Borders trip to Nepal, we were focusing on doing shows for young girls who had been victims of trafficking. Visiting one of the safe houses belonging to the organisation Maiti Nepal, we were going to do a show for 250 girls and their children. 45% of the girls were suffering from HIV and TB and most of them had been sold as early as the age of 12.

As I was changing into my costume in one of the classrooms and looking out of the window, I watched young women putting out chairs on one side of the stage. Even though most of them looked under 18, each had one or two children who were sitting on another side of the aisle on the ground. As I was looking at them, it struck me that there was no way I could ever understand what these young women had experienced. I could never imagine the nightmares they had survived. The question arose: what right did I have to come here and try to make them laugh?

Three minutes into the show, they're laughing so hard they're falling off their chairs, and I'm aware of not even being that funny. At that moment I realise that the more difficult situation the human being is experiencing, the more important it is for them to laugh. People who have experienced intense trauma actually have a physical need to find release, and laughter is one way of providing that sense of liberation.

IV

The Sweet Essence
of Clown

'It's not about acting stupid,
it's about daring to be perceived as stupid.'

Nalleslavski

Defining what 'clowning' is isn't the most simple
thing. The question must be asked, what are we
talking about when we talk about clowning? What is
a clown? Well, my first answer to this question would
be another question: in what context?

When I found my calling as a clown it was no longer
just about the performance situation and making
people laugh, it became something bigger. Seeing
through the eyes of the clown opened me up to the
world of clowning as a philosophy.

THE FIVE LAYERS OF CLOWN

I divide clowning into five fundamental layers which try to connect and separate the different layers of clown philosophy and clown tools:

1. Clown philosophy

2. Clown identity

3. Clown attributes

4. Clown performer

5. Clown tools

1.   Clown Philosophy

If you see life and performance through the eyes of the trickster, you'll be looking for ways to twist and spin other people's perspectives. Tricksters violate taboos and customs, have no regard for authority, and disrupt the established order, capsizing situations as they go.

For the purposes of this book, and in relation to clowning, I'm referring to the trickster archetype as the one in society whose function it is to turn the world upside down. The trickster figure turns the bad into good, the good into bad and reminds us that we are safe but we are never safe.

Having a prolonged mythical and cultural history, the trickster appears in multiple colourful stories worldwide. In Scandinavia we have Loki, in China the monkey king, in Christianity the devil. Many cultures have trickster animals like the coyote, raven, fox or the African hare (which inspired the creation of Bugs Bunny). The Navajo have a trickster who craps on the head of the chief who's being an asshole.

Since all tricksters have the mandate to turn the world upside down, in some extreme way, the thinking behind this could lead to the idea that Hitler and Jesus were clowns because they shifted the world order. Many people would be very opposed to perceiving Hitler and Jesus as clowns, but on a trickster/clown philosophy level, I do.

Clowns walk that fine line between order and disorder. They set up a norm and then break it, either intentionally or unintentionally.

When you're doing a solo show the dynamic of the game is about gaining control and losing control so sometimes you're failing and sometimes you're succeeding. There's a clown tradition of duos when one polarises this concept, where each clown takes a role. One takes the role of creating order (success) and the other creates chaos (failure). In the circus tradition we see it represented by the circus director or white clown, and the red clown or trickster (the drunk, the hobo) who creates disorder.

The idea is to create a tension and then create release. This is how we sculpt our art, by determining where these elements are. The white clown creates tension and the red clown provides release. The white clown needs the audience to take a moment seriously, and the red clown will fart. Tension and release, control and chaos, white clown and red clown, somehow they're all part of the same story. A teaching exercise I use to illustrate this concept is the 'Gibberish argument', where students argue whilst sliding up a scale of 1 – 10, ending with stage fighting (a slap). I've noticed people tend to resist building a situation to an emotional climax. It's a reflex, we're used to defusing the tension by telling a joke or undermining the emotionality of the situation in some way. Part of creating clown art is to try to keep the tension, and to have a sense of timing as to when the release needs to drop in, kickstarting the comedy.

'Everything for the clown is life or death'

Nalleslavski

The traditional view of the circus is that the circus performers are working with success and that the clowns work with failure. My feeling is that the modern performer should master both. The juggler should be able to find just as much material in the failure of the trick as in the success, and the clown should master the emotions of success just as they must master the emotions of failure.

If you allow yourself to fully inhabit the failures as well as the successes, you're in control since you can command a range of emotional outcomes. In order to do this, the circus performer has to run the risk of being perceived as stupid or incompetent, and the clown must dare to be brilliant.

Most people make the generalisation that just because the clown uses failure as a tool, they must always fail. Instead I use the concept of *catastrophe*, which in this case could be described as an emotional climax, a reversal of what is expected, leading to a turning point and resolution. This can translate to either success or failure. What is important is that the clown invests this ebullient or tragic moment with truthful hyper emotion. Things get funnier when you increase the stakes to catastrophic proportions.

Both comedy and tragedy are based on the truth of what it means to be a human being. The borderline between them is fragile. The clown possesses the freedom of switching between comic and tragic emotions, allowing the audience to release their tension by laughing at the clown's emotional vulnerability in the face of reality.

'Don't be funny. Be real.'

Nalleslavski

Many laughs have been created by children who are trying to fit into this world. It's funny when they use adult language or behaviours that so evidently reflect how they see the adult world around them. Wearing their parents' shoes, which are way too big, or commenting on subjects they clearly don't know anything about (yet ironically those comments can come across as so wise). We don't laugh at their stupidity, we laugh at their naivety as they try to do the right thing.

I believe the essence of clown is not 'stupidity'. It's not about acting stupid, but rather about daring to be perceived as stupid. The working term I use for stupidity is 'naivety'. This is the open-eyed viewing of a world much bigger than one's self, and the attempt to understand it. One of the secrets to naivety is simply *seeing*: reacting to whatever is real in each moment.

Naivety can be measured in the amount of time a character takes between the action and reaction. So for example, the more naive your clown is, the longer the moment between someone stepping on your foot and you realising it. The problem with the word 'stupidity' is that it's judgmental and can be difficult to actually play. If you are judging your character as stupid, you're already outside your character. Naivety, on the other hand, is a state of being that brings you into your character.

The strength of the clown is in being able to rediscover. With a sense of naivety, not knowing, you start with nothing but are forced into the action of discovery. As clowns we can learn from the child who has failed and been perceived as funny or stupid. The only difference is our awareness of having to create the failure, whereas the child just does it naturally.

2.   Clown Identity

Identifying yourself as a clown isn't always a matter of choice. Being labelled the class clown, one can either be oppressed by the label or accept it and relish in it, discovering tools along the way to make the class laugh. It seems that in any group situation, a clown emerges. Almost none of these people will actually become performers, yet they can still identify or be identified as clowns.

If an actor dresses up as a clown, are they a clown or an actor? The actor would probably say they're a clown, the clown would say they're an actor.

Performance genre and identity are usually very strongly connected. In the past, you couldn't go to a circus school to learn the trade. Either you were circus family or you weren't. This is no longer the case now that there are circus schools everywhere but the notion still persists in comedy. There's this idea that you're either funny or you're not – and in clowning especially it's very deeply rooted. People believe that you can't teach someone to be a clown.

Of course this isn't my perspective. I think anyone can be taught, can be given the tools to become a performing clown. But this doesn't mean I don't recognise the fact that there's this inherent identity of a 'clown'. A lot of people who aren't performers identify with the clown – they'll wear silly socks and try to make people laugh, though they may not be aware of the clown tools they're using.

3.   Clown Attributes

These are symbols that trigger people to identify something as clown. This can be different for different cultures.

Attributes are important because they are the code that tells the audience what to expect. In Myanmar a comedian will wear a farmer's hat. In Western society, if someone is wearing bright colours, a red nose and big shoes, the audience will expect them to be funny, or at least try to be funny.

There's a very strong American movement that believes as long as you use the Western clown attributes, you are a clown, which can be scary sometimes if the clown ends up enjoying themselves more than the audience does. Even though I identify them as clowns, I do not perceive them as performers who are using clown performance tools.

On the flip side, when parents hire someone trained at a European clown school they can be disappointed when the performer turns up without the costume of a 'traditional' clown.

Social codes and attributes aside, my belief is that the essence of the clown performer is always about being playful and connecting to an audience.

4.   Clown Performer

This layer refers to the actual job of performing for an audience, and the dialogue between clown and spectators in the context of the show.

Clowns don't start the story until they're in front of an audience. A good clown show has its own life, it should contain a structure for safety, but each show should feel like a unique meeting with that particular audience. A clown performer dedicates their lives to perfecting the experience for the audience and, I believe, the best clown shows get better and better with each performance.

My goal has always been to create a show that could work both at a refugee camp in Rwanda as well as in a corporate environment in Sweden. A show improves and benefits from being performed in different environments.

Clown performance doesn't necessarily happen only in the show, sometimes the most magic moments are playing with the children when you're putting on your make-up before the show, or after when you're saying goodbye.

5.   Clown Tools

This layer of clown contains the collected body of practical knowledge in the field of physical comedy. The main body of my *Nalleslavski Method* resides in this layer and anyone can use these tools for performance, whether they identify with or dress as clowns or not.

A clown's box of tools has many compartments. There are emotional tools such as hyper-emotionality, conceptual tools such as success and failure, the creation of order or chaos (or both, sometimes at the same time). Practical tools could include physically demonstrative tricks: knowing how to juggle, do acrobatics, tightrope walk and so on.

V
The Clown Manifesto

- **Everything is the Audience**

Without the audience my art form dies. I must therefore alter my focus from me as a performer to my audience and their experiences. The whole purpose of my art is to guide the audience through an emotional experience, they are the primary focus of the creative process.

One of the main techniques I teach for performers to connect with their audience is:

'Begin on a lower energy level than your audience so that you can tune into them. Catch up to their level and bring the audience with you to a climax.'

Climax is the key tool I have found that helps performers create catharsis for an audience. If a performer can involve the audience in their actions and keep their attention whilst building towards the situation's climax, the audience response is tangible. Performers must feel their emotional response building like a wave and hopefully ride it, giving both themselves and the audience an emotional experience.

Take the time to tune into the audience at the beginning so they can participate in your emotional journey instead of just being spectators. Your role is to lead them to an emotional catharsis. Catharsis derives from a Greek word meaning 'cleansing' or 'purging'. It was the Greek philosopher Aristotle who first introduced the word as a medical term describing the body's different cleansing or purging processes. Later, he used the term to describe the emotionally purifying effects an audience could experience while watching a tragic play.

My philosophy frames catharsis as any purging of emotion experienced by an audience, in relation to art. Catharsis is emotional cleansing, a release of pent-up emotion which can be set into motion by comedy as well as tragedy, and it is the performer's and clown's task to take their audiences to these emotional edges. No one can guarantee that your audience will allow themselves to dive into their emotions to the point that they come out the other side feeling released, but you can always make it your aim.

• Performer/Creator

Unlike traditional or normative structures which tend to view performers as tools for interpreting a director's or choreographer's artistic vision, I believe that performers are most inventive when we follow our own creative impulses and have the understanding and ability to influence the whole creative process. As much as possible, clowns should try to work from their own material, (and find creative collaborators along the way) with the specific aim of helping their audience experience emotions, to experience catharsis.

• Connect and Play

The only two qualities that I've come to find are fundamental to the essence of clowning, are *connect* and *play*. A clown's primary hunger is to get a response from the audience. You can look like a clown, but if you're not connecting and playing with the audience, it's not clowning. The flip side being that even if you aren't doing something that's traditionally perceived as clowning (such as theatre or ballet), but you are connecting with your audience and being playful, I would consider it clowning.

• Comfort the disturbed or disturb the comfortable

Answering this question not only gives you the social tools to do the right thing in the right situation, but it also gives you artistic power to know what goal you're trying to achieve. You have to understand who your audience is. Often it's a delicate dance between comforting and disturbing which has to be navigated with heightened sensitivity.

Another purpose of art from the *Nalleslavski* perspective, inspired by the role of the *Shaman*, is to balance society either by creating heart-warming laughter or by pushing audiences to a place they experience as unsettling, thought-provoking and challenging.

Every time you meet an audience you have to decide: is this audience disturbed and in need of comfort, or is it a comfortable audience which needs to be disturbed?

Within a hospital clowning situation or a Clowns Without Borders mission or even when performing for very small children, usually the concept of 'comforting the disturbed' applies. It's crucial to create an environment in which your audience feels comfortable enough to release their emotions. It's probably obvious to say, but don't go into a refugee camp and try to disturb the audience, rather aim to bring warm, healing laughter to people affected by trauma.

On the other hand, when performing within one's own culture, with people who are comfortable with the situation, such as in a black box European theatre, try to find ways of disturbing the audience's equilibrium, their sense of security and contentment. 'Disturbing' in this sense means a provocation which agitates someone in their comfort zone. You break their expectations, annoy their sense of ease in order to wake them up, to affect or move them, to give them an unexpected emotional experience.

My burlesque character *Cocobelle* exists in this realm, she is pure provocation. In the number 'Pink Perhaps', Cocobelle starts off singing in a gentle and scared way, and it ends with her pulling out pink feathers from her underwear and stapling them to her body whilst singing 'Fuck the Pain Away'.

- **Bag of Tricks**

There is a clown tradition where the clown enters the stage with a suitcase that is filled with their tricks. Personally I've built up my bag of tricks with non-verbal elements of magic, music, circus and puppetry, making me able to work in any audience situation anywhere in the world. Of course you don't actually need a suitcase, though it does give you a good excuse to visit all the city's second hand shops in search of the elusively 'right' bag for your clown.

- **Love Thyself**

On airline flights we learn to put on our own oxygen masks before we begin to help others. This applies strongly for performers whose work it is to give of themselves. In order to make others happy we must first understand our own happiness. To be of service fully, we must find ways of re-juicing our batteries, both within the performance but also in our lives. We owe it to our audiences and to ourselves.

Much more than physical exertion, I find what's most draining is stress and worry, usually around these three issues:

1. **The audience.**

Worries around being judged by the audience.

2. **Myself.**

Worries around whether my own physical and emotional capacities are good enough. Will I be able to hold the concentration levels, the emotional depths? Am I capable at this moment (especially if I'm performing a second show or haven't had enough time to warm up)? Will I be able to really be in the moment?

3. The room.

Will the practical things work: lights, sound, tricks. Are all props in their right place? Did I do the rigging properly?

'Love thyself' is the goal of feeling rejuvenated instead of drained after a show. So, how do we do this as performers? Firstly, a good measure of preparation before the show can help to reduce stress and worry. Make sure you have enough time to rig the stage, to set your props and check everything is in its right place. Ensure there is space for a warm-up of sorts. The shape of this is different for different people. Some need to be quiet, to meditate before a show, others need to do a full yoga class, juggle or play heavy metal and jump against walls. It doesn't matter what your method is, just do whatever you need to do to bring yourself into the present, into the zone. Each performer needs to discover their self-loving ritual before the show.

During the show find those moments of enjoyment and treasure them. For example, often on a Clowns Without Borders tour, it's very easy to feel drained due to not only the sheer amount of shows one has to do in a day, but also heat or miserable conditions; witnessing people in unfathomable situations or having to perform while battling diarrhoea. In spite of these intense situations, take advantage of that magical moment during the show when, just peeking through the curtain, you see the faces of the children laughing, and all of a sudden you feel energised again.

Between shows, be kind to yourself. Exercise, spend time in nature, find something joyous to do. Most importantly, build up the energy to enjoy the next show. The goal isn't just to make you feel good, the goal is to be a top notch performer. It's your responsibility to make sure your batteries are loaded for performance. You need to be able to give, since this is the clown's job. But the performer's job (in order to be a clown) is also to be able to receive. Can you dare to receive? This exchange will create a sense of vitality. Find what generates good energy for you and feel entitled to receive it.

VI

The Nalleslavski Method

'There are no bad audiences.'

Nalleslavski

Reflections on Connecting and Playing

Stacey: 'You know there's no such word as awarenesses?'

Nalle: 'There is now.'

To be able to do any of the work of a clown, you have to be able to come on stage, dare to stand still and to connect with an audience. You have to have the courage to play and to be aware within this playing that there is an audience watching you and sharing your experience. The goal of my method is to help performers develop more connected and playful relationships with their audiences.

As a performer I have spent years searching for the universal lowest common denominator of laughter. I have endlessly searched for underlying structures, trying to really understand the architecture of comedy, but every new situation and new audience changed the game just enough so that the structures I had previously built had to change as well. It was not until I started focusing on teaching that I really discovered what I feel is the core of clowning: to CONNECT and PLAY.

All of a sudden I realised the ever-changing game, never twice the same, could be simplified to a rule that not only generated a format to hold on to, but also fostered freedom of creativity. I had found my golden key.

For many years I taught one- to two-week workshops to actors, clowns, circus artists and corporate public speakers and observed that even though the golden key was discovered through my clowning, on a wider scale it was simply about working with live audiences and was, therefore, much more universally applicable than I had previously imagined.

CONNECT

'Make the audience feel seen.'

Nalleslavski

Since the audience is always the main focus within the creative process, performers should consistently have an awareness of how their audience is being affected. We have to get the audience to lean forward and engage with the show and become immersed with what's happening on stage. I believe the moment when the audience forgets where they are, 'the room turns red'. This is a theatrical term used to describe the moment the spectators become fully engaged with the show. Connecting with the audience is for me primarily the art of the dialogue.

When teaching, an exercise called 'the dialogue' is one of the first I usually start with. Students sit in pairs and I ask them to say hello and talk to each other as if they were complete strangers. Afterwards we reflect about what the patterns were and, most frequently, they are similar. Both took time to make sure the other person had a chance to participate. Both mixed taking focus and giving focus. Both had an awareness of whether the other person was engaged or not. If someone talked too long without reconnecting, the other person's interest started to waver. With regards to real communication, the social rule of not suppressing your dialogue partner is crucial, yet for some reason as soon as we stand on stage we often take for granted that it is ok to have a non-connecting monologue. It is easy for the performer to let their awareness of the stage action and their own internal dialogue be more important than their awareness of the audience. If the audience is sufficiently intrigued by the stage action then this is not a problem. If they are not enthralled, however, then you have lost them and they leave, either mentally or physically. The question is: as the performer, are you aware whether the audience is mesmerised or not? Are you connected to them? My teaching dilemma always focuses on how to consistently maintain our awarenesses whilst in dialogue with the audience. How do we do this whilst simultaneously focusing on the story, co-actors, improvisatory moments or seven balls in the air?

The levels of awareness I use are:

• the audience

• self (the performer's breath, energy and emotional levels, the shape and movements of their body)

• space (including the 'real' room, the actual stage as well as the performer's imaginative space or world)

• co-performers and volunteers

• props or objects on stage

• actions

• the dramaturgy of the material

• the audience. I mention them again because they deserve it.

My thinking is that we must both heighten our constant awareness of the audience and their reactions as well as build in 'reconnection bus stops' when we are creating material for our shows. These are breaks in the action where we have planned moments of audience reconnection.

Astute awareness of the audience, and the ability to play with this awareness, is for me a golden key of a brilliant performer. Of all the 'awarenesses', this game between performer and audience is by far the king of the equals. It is the most important element a performer needs to capture and hold their audience.

To expand their awarenesses in all directions, performers need to possess basic stage techniques such as making sure they can be seen and heard. It sounds simple, but it's crucial to be aware of what the audience is experiencing. The performer must be aware of the different variables that influence their performance. If you have good material but you don't know where your audience is or where you are in the room, it doesn't work.

It's important to be aware of the physical circumstances, such as the architecture of the room: is there a trapdoor, window or faucet which can be incorporated into the performance? With an enlarged awareness of the room, options will be so much more varied since all of these qualities become improvisational opportunities.

There really is a lot to think about when you are on stage, yet that is the very time performers should not be thinking at all. They should be connecting and playing.

The Nalleslavski Cinnamon Bun Dough Analogy

Training awareness reminds me of making cinnamon buns. When you make cinnamon buns, first you make a ball of dough. With a roller, you first roll the dough in one direction. When you change positions to roll in another direction, the first direction will recede, so you have to go back and roll over it again. It's important to keep on rolling and, the more directions you roll in, the bigger the dough becomes and the more it stays in all directions. And so the dough expands.

For me, this is exactly what we have to do with our awareness when on stage. We have to keep our attention on the audience, the room we're in and the material we're performing, all at the same time, whilst simultaneously being open to improvisational possibilities, those unplanned moments brimming with comedy gold. Without training, when we focus on the action we can easily disconnect from the audience, just as when we focus on the audience, it's possible to lose awareness of our co-performers or volunteer. When you go off in one direction, you lose another, but if you train your awareness by consistently going back, giving each level of awareness attention so that the whole can expand, the dough becomes delicious in the end.

CLOWN TOOLS for CONNECTING include:

Eye Contact

By eye contact I don't mean that blurry look into middle distance which you see so often on theatre stages, I mean using real eye contact. I feel the eyes are the windows to the soul and, when confronting a clown, the audience must truly feel seen.

Listening

It's also really important to listen for audience reactions, and to respond to these. When creating clown material remember it's a dialogue with the audience so leave spaces where the audience is supposed to be answering.

Bus Stops

Sometimes when I work with jugglers, I notice they're so focused on their juggling that they're not aware of the audience. Alternatively, sometimes they stare blankly at the audience; we can see that behind their eyes they are thinking about their next trick. A way to solve this is to add choreographed beats where they are connecting with the crowd just often enough so the audience feels connected the entire time. Mentally I find this also helps free the mind to really focus on the difficult juggling technique since there is no split focus. Do one, then the other...

Choreograph your Awarenesses

One of the problems with performing is that if you're not used to it, your focus is usually only in one place at a time. So when I start choreographing numbers I not only add beats which take in the audience but also beats of the other awarenesses like props, room, co-performers. For example, when you first enter a room take time to experience it, then connect your experience with the audience. If you sit in a chair, take time to experience it, then share that experience with the audience. Between each choreographed awareness reconnect with some audience awareness.

Being aware of where your focus is, isn't a revolutionary concept, but it's often forgotten. As a comic performer, I can learn to switch between these awarenesses more and more rapidly to humorous effect. Importantly, the performer must also be aware of their ability to steer where the audience is looking by choosing where to focus.

PLAY

'Dedicate yourself to the game, even if the game changes.'

Nalleslavski

Children are masters of play yet for some reason our culture has created a value system which encourages grown-ups to stop playing. Children play, adults do not.

When I ask children in refugee camps if they appreciated our show, one of the strongest comments I am usually given is, 'I have never seen a grown man play'. Serious times crave serious people yet those who study happiness say the opposite. People we perceive as happy are the ones who can stay playful during serious times. I describe playfulness as: *dedication to the game, even if the game changes.* So to play one must come up with games. Everything can be made into a game and the clearer the game is, the easier it is to dedicate oneself to it.

Clown workshops are generally held in game format where different games are used to train different elements of awareness, patterns or structures. Many students confuse playing the game with winning the game. When they perceive they are losing the game, they become filled with negative feelings.

Some clown pedagogues play on this and push this vulnerability since it too is a game that the audience finds entrancing. My feeling is that if one is being pushed to one's limitations, the lack of freedom to choose inhibits playfulness. Student performers can get too involved in their own tunnel-vision experience of going 'all in'. As a clown you have to 'focus wider', remember not to push one awareness at the expense of losing another. Sometimes going all in means losing the awareness of the game. Even though the clown may cross the line into the so-called 'real', they still need to be in the realm of playfulness. If you are just running and screaming, there's no game anymore. As I like to say, if you run too fast, it's hard to dance. This for me is no longer playful and therefore is not clowning... even if the audience is falling off their chairs laughing.

Something I like to research is how we can push emotional intensity without losing the freedom to play. How do we find our balance within the game of extremes? For example, if you're playing a scene where you're being hunted by monsters, don't begin with the emotion at 110% since this will limit your creative freedom, your options of expression will diminish and there will be less space for playing.

To clown is to fall in love with the game wholly, with one's body, mind and emotion. If you are furious at the door that will not open you must enjoy the moment to its fullest and of course not forget to reconnect and share the moment with your audience.

I have found that when performers play at 110% the game disappears. The secret is to fully invest in the game, but to not over-invest.

CLOWN TOOLS for PLAYING include:

You have to first decide what the imaginary situation is, clarify the idea for you and the audience and then play the game, developing it along the way.

Finding the game

The clown is right here, right now, discovering the world, unearthing things and making the audience laugh along the way. The question the audience wants to know is: what game are we playing? Sometimes the game is pre-determined, as in the clowns who are going to try and perform *Romeo and Juliet*, but a lot of clown training is based on being able to enter a room and not know what the game is, on discovering the game as it emerges. Many clown shows are a playful mix of both.

What is a game? A game could be an exploration of a phenomenon or a problem that has to be solved. A game needs enough rules so that you can play, but not so many as to hinder the playing.

Clarifying the game

When the audience understands what the game is, this increases their sense of involvement in the material, which is vital for the performer to be able to interactively play the game with them.

Distil the clowning game into a sentence describing something that must be either solved or explored.

Developing the game

With problems, develop the game by finding different attacks until you finally solve the problem. Alternatively, find patterns so the problem repeats itself. The game of exploration is usually self-developing, but in both, performers can create dramaturgy using various tools such as increasing levels of energy and emotion.

Dare to stick with the game and dare to let the game change

It's important to trust a game enough to dare to stick with it, to really be able to discover all the possibilities it can lead to, but also to dare to change it. Sometimes you choose to change it, but sometimes it's chosen for you, like when you are given a gift from the clown gods.

Exercises for playfulness:

The pre-determined game: Put your clown character into improvised pre-determined situations, eg. You are lost in the jungle, or the King addressing his subjects.

The non-pre-determined game: Enter the stage without any idea of what is going to happen, trusting fully that a game will emerge.

Nalleslavski's Triangle

I was given the opportunity to start my own school in the beautiful countryside outside of Stockholm; I called it The International School of Physical Comedy. My idea was to explore the tools that clowning had given me but to offer their lessons to a wider range of performance artists. Since the school was full time I also needed a bigger vision than the one I had for my shorter workshops. My vision became to create a school that mixed the free creativity of play with the structured creativity of creating one's own solo show.

To create a solo show, I realised I needed to find a new pedagogical structure, and after many years and multiple changes I now call this structure the *Nalleslavski Triangle*:

1. **World:** WHERE are you asking the audience to join you? It could be the world of the circus, underground with trolls or in the kitchen.

2. **Character:** WHO does the audience see you as on stage?

3. **Action:** WHAT do you do on stage? This could be juggling, singing or hunting a lion. The creation of action-based material can then be moulded into dramaturgy.

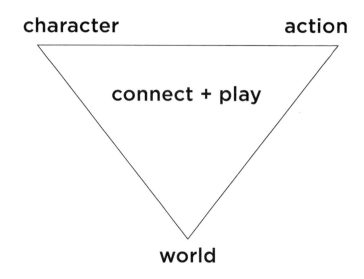

*The Nalleslavski
Triangle*

The solo show is important to me because in my world the variéte still rules. By 'variéte', I mean number-based routines. Whether for a Clowns without Borders expedition or for a corporate event, if a group of performers who each have their own solo material meet, they can create a magical show whilst having coffee. A group of performers who lack their own solo material will not be able to throw a show together easily. Of course they could make a show using a normal rehearsal process but in the professional world I work in, we are constantly being asked to perform without having the option of rehearsals. I love it! The best part is of course that after the first show the game of improvement is on and, since each performer has the safety net of their individual skills, they could actually in their own right do the show by themselves. And so the games can begin.

At the school, the idea of owning one's own solo show was a brilliant catalyst for creation. The creative energy of the class spurred everyone on, and the freedom of working solo kept the artistic process in the hands of the individual performer. It doesn't matter which part of the *Nalleslavski Triangle* you begin with, just begin where your ideas start. The most important thing is to clarify your initial impulse. You just need a key to be able to open the door, it could be an idea of a fun character, an old lady. Or you could want to create a show based on a new magic trick, or you have a post-apocalyptic world you want to create on stage. Importantly, in some way your show should have elements of all three parts.

WORLD:

Personally I like starting with the WORLD of the show. It is the easiest way for me to quickly jump into a new creative process. I divide the world into what is known to be real and what is imaginary.

- The Real World refers to the actual situation I will be performing in. It's important to know what the performance space will be and who the potential audience is.

For example, a performance space could be a street in a busy European square, a fancy up-market theatre, or a dilapidated soccer pitch in a Congolese refugee camp. Your audience would obviously differ with each space, they could be drunk strangers, families or refugee children. What is important, at this point, is that once you know the 'real' world in which your show will be performed, you research and assess any cultural or social elements that might be relevant. For instance, if you're part of a Clowns Without Borders expedition performing in Rwanda, it's helpful to know that having an excessive amount of make-up/paint on your face may send unintentional signals to the audience. In that context, face-painting sometimes symbolises a sign of war or conflict. Because of these specificities, it's important to research your audience's cultural background and to acquaint yourself with some of that culture's basic belief systems.

Right from the start, it helps to quickly assess what one knows and doesn't know about the real world one will be performing in. Limitations can be the best way to kick-start creativity. This is also the stage when you decide whether you want to create a show that comforts the disturbed, or disturbs the comfortable.

- The Imaginary World, on the other hand, is what we create, the world we invite the audience to enter. This world allows the spectators to suspend their disbelief, to momentarily forget that they are still in the so-called real world. It helps them access their playfulness. It is also a reference that can quickly help a creative process.

For instance, I had a dream of creating a show in the world of Moulin Rouge. I envisioned the Real World it would be performed in would be fancy spaces where the audience is eating a three-course dinner – a standard corporate event setting in Sweden. For this concept, I created the Imaginary World of *Moulin Noir*, a failed Parisian night club, where none of the other artists show up so I have to perform all the numbers myself. As soon as the idea for the world was set, the objects, situations and characters that fitted into it became very clear.

In creating a WORLD there are only two reactions your audience can have:

– they're either leaning in towards you and entering your world, or

– they're leaning away from you and are feeling excluded or are excluding themselves from your world.

One of the easiest ways to lose the audience is by making them feel that they don't understand the context of what they're watching. Alternatively, they might not be interested in that context. If the clown's material doesn't evolve, if it stays static for too long with regards to tempo/energy or content, the audience will slowly start pulling away, leaving your world. That's why when creating a show, it's important to create a context or world the audience can agree to believe in and understand. Within this world, your material should be dynamic enough to keep them engaged for the entire show.

Caution: beware of the gag!

The gag can kill 'the world'. It may provide a temporary moment of release, or undermine the action and reveal the performer's ironic intelligence, but in the end it can destroy the world you have carefully constructed for the audience.

Example:

*In my clown trio show **Drömställe** ('Dream place'), we play three white beautiful bird-like creatures who, through their own longing, have trapped themselves in a huge golden bird cage. Since this is a clowning show, we spent a lot of energy in the rehearsal process*

playing with how funny it would be to walk in and out of the cage we were trapped in. But soon we realised the gag of walking out of the cage could kill the tragic game we were playing of being trapped within it, and that it was more important to keep the magical world we had created than get the quick laugh. Of course now that the show has been tested and we know that the audience does get drawn into our world, I really feel like experimenting with how much we can break the rules of the game we have set up, yet keep the world. Is it possible for all three of us to leave the cage, possibly even going and sitting in the audience, asking them for help and advice on how best to escape from the cage?

Drömställe

Photograph © Jean-Paul Bichard

In writing this book I realise just how important **WORLD** has been in my creative processes. *The Burnt Out Punks* is my show with the widest audience reach. It is Europe's largest touring pyrotechnical circus and we do massive shows for up to 12000 people at a time.

I'm so proud of this crazy punk circus and how we seem to be able to affect audiences profoundly wherever we go. It's a burning post-apocalyptic world where an eclectic bunch of punk characters live and tour in an old Scania bus from 1963.

I think humans have the inherent need to completely let go of all control every now and then. Some cultures have the Carnival, in Sweden we have alcohol on a Friday night. *The Burnt Out Punks* is a controlled version of creating utter chaos but within a harness of love, warmth and laughter. Our show isn't negative, there's no malice in it; we call ourselves 'jackasses with heart' as we blow ourselves up laughing hysterically. We're mixing the best of the catastrophe with the best of the orgasmic climax and doing them at the same time. Everything goes wrong, and we love it.

When the audience leaves our show I believe that the sum of the show is larger than all the tricks we have performed, it is a complete world we have shared with them.

CHARACTER

> '**Just because the audience is laughing,
> it does not mean that they like you
> or what you are doing.**'
>
> *Nalleslavski*

CATEGORIES OF CHARACTER:

– Playing someone else (acting)

– Playing yourself (being)

– Introvert (focused on action)

The first entrance of the clown is about letting the audience see you, it's not about the story. Performers must know how they are being perceived by their audience. In Commedia dell'arte there is a technique where the character must stop as soon as they enter the stage, stopping all action to connect with the audience and to give them time to see who is on stage. If the human being judges and places each new person they meet within the first seven seconds of meeting them, then upon the entrance is when we give the audience these seconds.

In Commedia this character is supported by the style of their entrance: the shape of their standing pose, their costume and their voice. Modern acting character work spends a lot of focus on the actor discovering who they think their character is. Using clown techniques we can spend an equal amount of focus on steering how the audience experiences our character.

As opposed to actor training where the focus is on portraying someone other than yourself, a lot of clown training is trying to understand how the audience perceives the performer. The work of clown character for me combines both of these views, a good clown persona is a combination of your private self as well as something other than yourself. When helping people find clown characters I have found sometimes it's easier to go one way or the other in order to reach this.

For example, is the person performing freed by being themselves more, by performing a character other than themselves, or by doing neither, taking away the personality and purely doing tricks? My teaching and directing experience has led me to divide performers into these three groups when it comes to character work. Depending on the individual, I will start helping them create their on-stage character or persona from one of these three approaches.

Playing someone else (acting)

'Playing someone else' is more of a traditional acting approach where the character becomes a mask that the performer wears. Most times I believe it's more important to maintain a level of playfulness as opposed to having a clear character. Sometimes when a character becomes locked too early, their playfulness can become limited. Jacques Lecoq once told me that a character should never limit themselves if the scene requires something more. For instance, if you are playing an old character and the scene needs you to climb a tall ladder, the performer might claim their character would never climb a ladder at that age. But wouldn't it be brilliant to see someone very old climb a ladder? The character work helps you discover how to climb it. Always let the needs of the scene steer the character.

Example: Inferno

Many of my characters are just me with a costume. The *Shaman*, my first character in *Burnt Out Punks*, never felt like an external character.

Besides the obvious externals, the *Shaman* was me working more non-verbally and in a much bigger scale (in front of 4000 to 6000 people) than my Clowns Without Borders character *Nalle Blue*. Due to needs within the show, *Shaman* has now transformed into *Inferno*, who's more camp, more flamboyant and has an English accent. The *Shaman* was initially a background character, but *Inferno* became the show's Master of Ceremonies. With the *Burnt Out Punks'* costume designer, we came up with the concept of a devil circus director. The situation called for something other than myself, and *Inferno* was born.

SHAMAN

Photograph © Mieszko Tyszkiewicz

Inferno has enlarged physical and vocal attributes, he's a megalomaniac who has visions of grandeur, he feels he owns the world. How he reflects on the world and acts within it is very different to who I am personally. (I hear my friends laughing in the background.)

INFERNO

Photograph © Martin Lundström

Because the character is further away from myself, I feel free to push his boundaries because it's not a reflection on who I am personally. I can dare to let him have tantrums and know that it'll work because it's who he is. In some ways I have less control over him. As *Inferno* I have a script I don't stick to. I know the gist of what the text is supposed to do, but within that the journey can be different each show. I need to not push on stage, just stand there and get that first applause. As soon as that happens it's, 'Ok let's go!'

In terms of character work for *Inferno*, I have made conscious choices. My animal for him is the peacock. My element is water. His triangle of traits are – hyper-emotional, flamboyant and sexual. His naivety I would say is on the level of a five year old, and he thinks he has everything figured out but then everything goes wrong. The costume's red high-heeled pumps really help me get into character.

Playing yourself (being)

Most trick-based performers, magicians and stand-up comedians usually belong to this group. The better you know yourself, the more you will understand how the audience is perceiving you.

Many performers are billed under their private name, yet most would say that when they are on stage they have a stage persona. I call this 'playing yourself (being)'. When becoming a performer, a lot of the character-creation process is understanding how the audience is perceiving you. I feel that much actor training is based on eradicating yourself to be able to enter another character, and this can be detrimental to the world of the clown. Your ticks, patterns and habits are your strengths and they should be enhanced and used as tools, not eradicated and looked down upon. You are what is interesting.

In this category it's important to see oneself from the perspective of the society one's performing for, taking into account personal elements such as appearance, emotional state, comportment, etc. as well as cultural specifications such as age, gender, ethnicity, class, and so on.

Usually we are performing for others within our

own social bubble so we forget the possibility that the audience is seeing something other than what we think they are seeing when they look at us. For years, inspired by my first clown teacher, I tried being aggressive towards my audience. Her whole essence was to provoke audiences. What took me a long time to understand was that I am not a small Italian woman. Large aggressive white males just don't get those belly laughs I was looking for. Then I started working with low status, which really taught me to connect with my audiences, but for years performing in Clowns without Borders situations I was having a hard time calibrating my performances. Whatever I thought I was doing, audiences had trouble perceiving a large white man as low status. Just the colour of my skin and what was imagined to be between my legs was affecting my communication whether I wanted it to or not. The only solution to this in my view is to just keep on being aware of it and to trust how the audiences are reacting as opposed to pushing how one thinks they should be reacting.

Example: Nalle Blue

Nalle Blue is the character I've been performing during all my years of working with Clowns Without Borders.

Essentially, *Nalle Blue* does not exist separately from myself, he's me with a costume on. As a trademark, he's a really cool poster and he's been performing for 15 years. Wearing an oversized hat and tails, sometimes I try to be more naive and sometimes I try to be more sly. Either way, I feel the audience experiences *Nalle Blue* as real, but personally I feel it's just me being playful.

I'm wearing a costume but the person on stage is no different to me playing with kids before or after the show. In many places the clown nose doesn't work so I've tried really bushy eyebrows or clown haircuts, but it isn't the externals that make me more playful. Playfulness comes mostly from the material, the magic, juggling or the mistakes I make. It comes from the audience's reaction or being chased by a dog in the middle of a show.

Photograph © Johannes Frandsen   *NALLE BLUE*

Introvert (focused on action)

High-level trick performers can often get stuck in character work that actually ruins or lessens the already magical quality of their actions. This happens a lot in new circus where a highly technically proficient performer tries to be creative with character, but in reality they just end up spoiling their trick material. In this case I encourage them to trust the focus on the action elements of the *Nalleslavski Triangle*. The work is based closely on the essence of the performer as a skilled artist. For example, when we watch an aerial hoop performer, the audience still realises that they are watching a person but they are primarily focused on the performer's movements or tricks.

Example: My work as a close-up magician

After years of directing magic shows and acts I have been smitten by the magic bug. Standing on stage is something I trust myself with so it has been easy to incorporate stage magic into my life; I feel I have the tools to make the tricks work since I already have the tools necessary to perform on stage. What I struggle with now is close-up magic as being very close to the audience really limits my ability to play with world and character. Working in the lap of the audience seems to force the need for extreme clarity and focus on the action. It is almost like I need to keep tabs on the size of my own persona so that it does not repeatedly upstage what I wish the audience to experience, the trick. So doing close-up magic is a brilliant opportunity for me to actively work on introverting my stage persona to help keep the audience focused on what I choose to have them focus on.

This of course can be seen all the time in the performing world of say classical musicians. Here the norm is that it's the art that is important and not the artist. The most important thing for me is to teach that it is always a choice and that there are tools to achieve either outcome one wishes for.

Whichever category of character you begin experimenting with, what's most important is not to get stuck in one category, but to use the three choices to investigate what frees you enough to play and connect with the audience. Once you make a decision, endless options open up concerning how to explore and design your character or non-character. Importantly, maintain a strong belief in the game you're playing.

Creating characters means asking questions, improvising and then making choices to gain knowledge of who the character is and who it is not, even if it is your own self.

CLOWN TOOLS for CREATING CHARACTER:

Scales

Almost anything that can be divided into variables can exist on a scale of 0 to 10. 0 to 6 is controlled, 7 to 10 is loss of control. For example, in relation to playing happiness, 0 would be the absence of happiness, and 10 would be ultimate bliss, yet at 7 I would say you're so happy that 'your ass leaves the chair'.

A performer must have what I call 'punch' – that ability to go into a bar where people don't care about what you're doing, and to get those at the back to become interested. The performer's levels of tension and energy, or elasticity, are what give 'punch' to a performer. The problem is that if you have full punch all the time there is no dynamic, therefore I use the concept of scales.

From a *Nalleslavski* perspective, what I'm really good at is the initial meeting with an audience, but less good with the 7 to 10 scale. For some reason I find it difficult to really let the madness go, to truly lose control. Perhaps I'm too aware of it from the outside, too conscious of the audience's response. I spend a lot of time being aware of the variables, but am at a point in my career where I should start to just let go and find the flow. My dream is to one day find the tools within myself to lose more control when I'm on stage and therefore to not just evoke warm nice laughter, but also create total chaos and hysterical mayhem in the audience.

Your zero

A lot of clown training is about discovering who you are on stage, through your own eyes as well as the eyes of the audience. Whatever category of character one is working with, the first step is to find your character's zero: the place of rest that the essence of your character comes back to when there is no action. The clearer the zero is to the performer, the easier it is to push the character to extremes. Finding a zero is creating a set of internal 0-10 variables like energy, rhythm, naivety, status or whatever feels relevant when deciding where one rests on the scale.

For instance, privately I perceive myself as a large tractor. I am normally quite slow and controlled. I can go fast but it takes me a while to pick up speed and then it is very difficult for me to change direction. I perceive my energy privately as being 3-4 on a scale of ten. Through years of clowning I have learnt that, when entering on stage, I should place myself at 4-5, just above my normal level to best connect and play. Not all performers should add energy. Some need to lower their level and some are perfect and just need to know it.

Energy

Energy is action or anticipation of action. The best way to describe energy for me is the exercise of introvert/extrovert.

In front of the class, stand neutrally and focus your mind on yourself, in an introverted way. Slowly become aware of the space where your feet meet the floor. Extend your focus and become aware of the audience who is looking at you. Usually this creates a natural heightened energy level in the performer.

I then create a scale: introvert 10-to-0 and then 0-to-10 extrovert. Whilst counting 10 to 0, the students focus on going from extreme introvert to extreme extrovert. Once they find a comfortable extreme extrovert placement on the 0-10 scale I then ask the student to continue holding the energy of that placement, but to shift their focus from introvert to extrovert. What becomes clear is the level of energy, and that can be effectively controlled by the performer.

Rhythm

Rhythm is the pace of one's actions or the space between one's actions. It can be connected to energy but could just as well be separate as when someone is totally calm but with an efficient quickness of rhythm.

The easiest way for me to explain rhythm is through music. What music do you connect to your character? A simple exercise is to have someone enter the stage humming the rhythm of their internal beat. This would be their rhythmic zero. From the outside it is then easy to encourage them to shift their rhythm by asking them to alter the frequency of the beat they are humming.

Like with all scales, characters must never get locked in one position. The zero is the resting place of the character; they can then start exploring the rest of the scale depending on the situation.

Naivety

Different aspects of the character's personality can be discovered by exploring them at different ages and this helps calibrate the character's level of naivety or experience.

An exercise is simply to lie on the ground, wake up as a newborn child and over 10 minutes age one year per minute, finishing with returning to the age you enjoyed the most and exploring it. This exercise can be used to find a clown, or to enrich the knowledge of your existing clown's naivety.

Naivety is based largely on your knowledge of the world. Is the world bigger or smaller than you are? If the world is bigger than you are it is easier to experience wonder, surprise and things beyond your understanding. It is connected to intelligence but I find intelligence difficult to play. To play dumb or smart can easily become playing a judgment about oneself which is intellectual. If a moment doesn't work I find it is because the idea has stayed on an intellectual level as opposed to being physically embodied. Ideas can come from the head, but need to land in the body and the situation. From the outside we of course judge the character. A character's 'stupidity' is measured by the time it takes from when a heavy object hits their foot to them realizing it and reacting. But playing stupid is a non-action. It gets stuck in the head instead of the body. I think finding your character's naivety is a great way around this.

Status

Status refers to where you belong on the hierarchy of power. A character's status can be shown in their relationships with other performers, their audience or even inanimate objects. Comedy potential lies in having opposing status relationships at one time. An example of this could be the servant in Commedia dell'arte, who switches between high status in relation to the audience and low status in relation to their master. This is what I call a 'status flip'.

Look at what your character's perceived social status would be, are they a prince or a cleaner? To make this more dynamic, ask the question: is the character hunting or being hunted? This is not necessarily dependent on social standing. A prince perceived to be high status can feel hunted or a cleaner can be hunting.

In relation to the audience, one of my favourite ways to distil a character's status is to ask 'the love questions'. Framing 'me' as the character and 'you' as the audience, the performer must decide what key love questions their character asks. Graphically, this could be represented as:

Do I love you?   Do you love me?

I love you   You love me

I'm not sure if I love you   I'm not sure if you love me

I don't love you   You don't love me

Using these questions, we can see that a character who confidently claims, 'I love the audience and the audience loves me' has a very different status relationship with their audience as opposed to the insecurity of one who wonders, 'I love the audience but I'm not sure if the audience loves me?'

Hungers

Simply put, in the Stanislavski system of performance, characters are driven by their super objective as well as by a bunch of mini or sub-objectives along the way. As performers who are clowns, our work is often character-based and not story-based. We therefore use similar tools to create motivations as those derived from Commedia dell'arte training.

Hungers are basically a character's main goal, they define their reason for being. The 'hunger' could be to get sex, food, money, power or even love from the audience. Hungers can change but not until they are satisfied, and they usually come back again. A character who is hungry for food and finally manages to sneak into the kitchen can eat until she/he is full, but in the next scene when they see an audience member with popcorn, the hunger must return. In this way, 'Hungers' make characters instantly recognisable, and should be consistently reinforced by the character's behaviour.

The triangle of traits

Basic commedia dell'arte characters can play with three major character traits which they have explored individually. For example, the servant Harlequino might have lazy, hungry and horny. He will spend most of his stage time jumping between these traits to create comedy.

In the process of discovering a clown's persona, one could start with exploring what you perceive as your three strongest personal traits. So for example, my personal traits could be that I'm loud, sensitive and a diva. After many years of performing, these have settled and are reflected in my characters' primary traits as extravagant, emotional and effeminate. At first it's important to delve into each trait individually, as a self-contained element. Each one is a key to a world where one can play and explore. The next step is to discover the play in-between these peculiarities. What's interesting with the clown is its ability to jump from trait to trait without a rational reason.

An exercise I use for jumping between qualities is that everyone is at a cocktail party where each character starts with one of their traits. Every time you meet a different character, you are forced to switch between your three traits.

Finally, when a character starts taking on a life of his/her own, it's often time to redefine what the triangle of traits is, taking into account the multiple ways in which the emotionality and physicality of the persona are developing.

Being Physically Emotional

> **'Physical comedy is when emotion becomes geographical.'**
>
> *Nalleslavski*

When you enter the world of the clown you realise the clown not only loves to have emotions, but adores sharing them with the audience. My suggestion is to have a food fight with emotion. When I teach, I make the students improvise very simple scenes in which I show them how to build stepping stones of emotion, how to keep their bodies in the emotion, letting the emotion build (which I call 'slow-burn') and then when reaching a 7 to 10 level of emotion, the performer loses control and allows the emotional explosion.

It is my belief that audiences get huge joy from watching a clown receiving an impulse, a 'trigger', that forces a physical reaction. A lot of clown training consists of getting the performer to delve into the joy of expressing emotion.

A tool to strengthen the effect of an expressed emotion for an audience is to make it three-dimensional by connecting it to the room. Like a camera might zoom closer to the face, the performer can choose to start an emotional scale far back on the stage and, as it's increasing, move towards the audience. It's entertaining to watch a clown's emotion becoming geographical in the way it connects to the physical room.

The way to make these games concrete is to link geographical variables in the room to emotional scales. This can also apply to other characters, for example someone becomes associated with 'angry', so the closer the performer's character gets to this person, the more they hurl abuse or become agitated. In this way you can use a character's blocking to inform their emotional content.

Ticks

We all have small private ticks that we are more or less conscious of. It could be blinking in a certain way or picking fluff off your clothes. Ticks are a great clown tool when they work. They are small reminders for the performer as well as the audience of the essence of the character. For example, a vain character could constantly be fixing their hair. The goal is to find one or two good ticks for every character. Try them out and see if the audience laughs. If they don't, simply try another one. Sometimes ticks can also be built into costume. A classic is the Turkish red fez hat with the over-long tassel rope hanging from the top. Every time the character leans forward, the rope gets in the character's face and makes them move it back again.

Costume

> **'If you can build a bag of tricks into your costume you always know you have them with you.'**
>
> *Nalleslavski*

For me, it's important the costume is part of the experience we're sharing with the audience, it must take them into a world. Beautiful and dramatic stage costumes will heighten the audience's overall experience whereas a poorly created costume will weaken their experience. Of course, a lot here is a question of taste, but it's good to remember that the costume is supposed to allow the audience to see the character more, as opposed to giving too many messages, which results in confusion.

A clown's costume should look professionally designed, and should have two or maximum three layers of information in colour and design. A mistake people often make with clown costumes is that they create chaotic, multi-layered outfits which in the end cancel themselves out; they're wearing fifteen different colours or patterns with their underwear on the outside, and the audience doesn't really understand what they're looking at.

Many performers are inclined to passively wear costumes and to not do anything with them. The costume needs to affect the performer and I would advise you to build a bag of tools into the costume's concept; that way you'll always have it with you.

Example: discovering COCO BELLE through costume

I went into a transvestite store once in Berlin, and bought 17cm high-heeled shoes with a red rose on them, and a pair of pink feather slippers. I took these shoes to my fabulous costume designer Helena and she made costumes for them based on my request to make them 'timeless classy' yet also make them somehow fit my body.

Coco Belle is me with high-heeled shoes or pink slippers on... and nipple tassles and hair curlers. At the moment, she's just me with two sets of clothes. I never talk to the audience before or after the set. I come on, sing my four-minute music routines, and leave. The 'Black Magic Woman' costume makes me feel like a buxom black woman, and the 'Pink Perhaps' costume makes me feel like a skinny white housewife, yet both come under the alias of *Coco Belle*. It's a costume-based routine in which I fill the mask of the costume.

What's nice about *Coco Belle* is that there's something about her that has a kind of socially loaded danger but that has a different effect depending on where I perform her. If I'm at a queer burlesque club, there's a sexualisation of the performance and people love it. In Poland I've had people laugh and then throw beer bottles at me, whereas at a dinner party for a company in Stockholm they think, 'He's so crazy!' and fully engage with her.

For some reason it's still loaded to see a man in high heels, especially if it's a fat man who seems to love what he's doing. There's no hiding behind the clothes, I'm clearly a man in woman's clothes. This is clowning, the audience can see through the drag persona, and see the big guy standing behind the microphone, the one who's just having a fun time singing and wearing high-heeled shoes.

COCO BELLE in 'Pink Perhaps'

Photograph © Maritin Lundström

ACTION
1. **Creating Material and Filling Your Bag of Tricks**
2. **Structuring Material to Create Emotional Orgasms**
3. **Improvisation and Gifts from the Clown Gods**

Creating Material and Filling Your Bag of Tricks

In Western clown school traditions, clowning is

often taught through character. My perspective is that this won't guarantee you a professional career or secure laughter from an audience. Instead, create physical comedy material from other starting points such as content, and then pool your material to create a show. It is my experience that character, if that's what you're looking for, tends to develop along the way.

The following table is a way of starting to develop material and fill your bag of tricks:

CREATE AN IMAGINARY WORLD your character can live in.

CATALOGUE SITUATIONS that could occur in that world

CATALOGUE THE OBJECTS that could exist in that world.

ASSEMBLE THE MATERIAL: collect and formulate it into numbers, routines, acts and shows.

1. CREATE AN IMAGINARY WORLD
    your character can live in.
    Play around with different possible environments in which your character can exist. Spend time playing there.

2. CATALOGUE SITUATIONS
    that could occur in that world.
    Choose simple situational ideas and improvise around them.
    Create slapstick material based on the situations failing and succeeding. Slapstick is based on the concept of: learn to do something right, divide it

into its different stages and parts, and then find ways to fail and succeed in each part.

The number three is important in comedy. One of the reasons for this is connected to the golden rule of comedy: to break or switch a reality (and to create the surprise necessary for humour), we have to understand what the reality is. The first two beats create knowledge, a believable world, a 'norm', which is broken or interrupted by the third beat. To clarify this even further:

Beat one shows us what is normal.

Beat two repeats what is normal so we trust that it is so.

Beat three breaks or switches what is normal to something different.

For example, when I teach slapstick I tend to begin with this slapstick routine. In pairs the students decide who is A and B. A slaps B, A slaps B, A slaps B but B ducks making A continue in a full circle. B then slaps A. It's the most simple routine, but done properly it can be funny every time.

3.   CATALOGUE THE OBJECTS
      that could exist in that world.
      For a clown, objects are a three-dimensional playground, but the main point is discovering how you play with any object. Decide which objects belong in your world and create material with them using:

• improvisation

• object manipulation which could involve juggling, magic or puppetry, and

• slapstick

Put very simply, juggling is the knowledge of playing with objects. Jugglers can dedicate themselves to how many objects they can keep in the air, but that's only part of their knowledge. Object manipulation is a huge part of the juggling world. The hard part is to find ways of using it without getting stuck in the form of only being a juggler, unless of course that's your choice. But the more juggling rule knowledge you have, the easier it is to start creating new material. Playing with an everyday object is great, preferably something you already have in your show.

Using simple magic tricks is a very good way of building up your bag of tricks. Some people don't realise how valuable it can be to learn just a few basic tricks. Go out there and find some to include in your show.

A very basic rule applies in puppetry: if you see the puppet, and you believe in it, the audience will see it and they will believe in it too. We are trained as a species to look for human characteristics in objects. In the most mundane of objects we can see faces and bodies with expression.

Create slapstick situations by playing with the correct use of the objects as well as the failure.

When teaching slapstick, I use an exercise called:

The chair

Sit on a chair. Analyse how to sit on a chair. Experiment with what could go wrong.
Come up with 5-8 ways of not sitting in a chair. Choose two good ones and create a sequence of fail, fail and then succeed. Remember that the intent must be clear from the beginning.

The clearer your intention is, the clearer the failure.

4.   ASSEMBLE THE MATERIAL:
collect and formulate into numbers, routines, acts and shows.

a. It's possible to structure material in many ways, one of which is based on storytelling or dramaturgy involving a story line, plot and a specific order of routines and gags. Remember to not let the gag get in the way of the dramaturgy.

b. Another way of ordering routines would be to use the concept of bus stops and beats.

Bus stops are the X on the map, they are dramaturgical points in the action for specific purposes such as creating a picture on stage, a tableau, or giving the audience the chance to react or breathe.

Beats are sequences of actions based on the notion of cause and effect. When one is finished, the next one starts.

The difference between beats and bus stops is simple; if a piece is choreographed in detail, it's choreographed in beats. Bus stops are bigger. You either have material that is 'beated' or material that is 'bus-stopped'. Both are structuring devices; they're triggers for new action, or stops after which something else happens. For example, in a juggling show, always consider putting a beat of audience connection before the final trick, which could be the last bus stop.

c. Loops are sequences of material that can be repeated ad infinitum. You take off your hat and bow to the audience. Your tie gets caught in your hat on the way up so it covers your face. Pause. Pull down the tie. You bow again. Repeat the tie action. Loops are a great way of building momentum on stage. Always try and see if your material can be restructured to loop.

Structuring Material to Create Emotional Orgasms

If you think of a performer's tension, energy or emotional levels in scales from 0 to 10, one of the ways of making material dynamic is morphing it with these scales in mind. In this way a performer's dynamism can mould and give texture to the material.

After the material is structured, adding beats where the audience can react helps build the momentum of the scene to an emotional climax. For example:

– enter the stage

– connect with the audience

– perform an action with a defined ending

– take in the audience's reaction

– respond to the audience's reaction by performing another action that is larger or stronger than the first one

– take in the audience's reaction again

– through a series of escalating steps which culminate in a climax, finally lead the audience to their emotional orgasm

– exit

Easy!

Improvisation and Gifts from the Clown Gods

> **'Check out the room before you perform, and plan all the good ideas you're going to spontaneously come up with.'**
>
> *Nalleslavski*

Improvisation comes into play from the moment we move from the classroom/rehearsal room onto the stage. This is the performer's chance to free themselves from the material, to be 'on' the moment, improvising and accepting gifts from the clown gods.

Endless literature exists about how important it is to be 'in' the moment, both in life and on stage. The real challenge as a performer is not only to be 'in' a moment, but to be 'on' it. As a performer and clown you have to remain open, listening attentively and responding truthfully. Being on the moment means not only being in it and experiencing it but also having the presence of mind to stay in the game, listening to the audience's response and incorporating any unexpected events.

Once the performer has a bag of tricks, improvisation is what connects them to everything and everyone: to the objects, the audience, the room, their co-performers and so on. My mask teacher Bruce at the Dell'Arte school in California, used to say:

> **'Luck is the residue of design.'**
>
> *(Bruce Marrs)*

It's a brilliant idea which I always apply to performing and life in general. When I arrive to perform in a space I've never seen before, the first thing I do is check out the room and figure out interesting ways I can use it. Perhaps there's a window I can climb out of or an elevated area off which I can fall. These are examples of planning spontaneity, where the gift is in the space that already exists.

Apart from planning a surprise, there will always be something unexpected happening in your show. For clowns these accidents are real gifts, they throw obstacles at us which can be transformed into opportunities. The woman with the hyena laugh in the third row, the person standing up to go to the toilet, or a sudden explosive sneeze in the auditorium. Knowing when to seize the moment is the mark of an exceptionally gifted performer. The mistake turns out to be a gift, it gives the performer or clown an opportunity to connect with their audience in an even more profound way. These accidents during the performance are what I would call 'gifts from the clown gods'.

The better your material, the stronger your character, the finer your skill set, the more chances you'll have of receiving gifts from the clown gods. I don't know who came up with the 'clown god' concept, I've never made a picture of what the clown gods look like, but I have seen someone talking into a microphone and the speaker falling down. The question is what do you do with that moment? If you're 'on' the moment, you can turn this mishap into comedy gold.

When teaching clowning I try to make 'catastrophe' the goal of every improvisation. *Catastrophe* is a beautiful word which has meant a lot to me. Throughout my clowning career, performing in areas struck by catastrophe, as well as performing for anybody personally struck by catastrophe, I have witnessed the internationally recognisable ordeal of the individual dealing with extremity.

Somewhere down the line, I heard that the Greek origin of the word 'catastrophe' does not only mean a negative climax but also the ultimate positive turning point as well, such as everybody getting married in the end, instead of everybody dying (though, done effectively, that can also be funny). I always urge improvisations to culminate in some sort of catastrophe, a situation where the stakes are enormous and the emotions heightened to their most extreme degree.

Love Your Volunteer

'Love your volunteer and your audience will love you.'

Nalleslavski

As flock animals, one of the biggest fears we have is being shunned from the group. To stand in front of a group and face the possibility of failure is, as far as I have discovered, an international anxiety-creating or even terror-provoking human experience. Using volunteers is asking someone to meet one of their biggest primal fears. Of course audience members do not want to join you on stage. If they do then you have probably chosen the wrong volunteer.

Using volunteers is an art form in itself. There are many reasons to use volunteers in a show and a few reasons why not. The primary reason to invite someone onto the stage is to create an instant link between the stage and the audience. The volunteer becomes the ambassador of the audience and amplifies their experience of what's happening onstage. Using a volunteer correctly immediately puts the audience on its toes for they too could soon be included in the show. This can be terrifying for some people. The recognition of the volunteer's fate and the distress of also being included is genuinely felt amongst all.

A big part of performer training is therefore just getting used to this situation and managing the energy it creates. I've seen too many performers using their volunteers incompetently, when they could be constructively employing the energy that volunteers create.

Secondary reasons for using volunteers could be the need to pad out a routine and make it longer, that you do not have enough hands and practically need help on stage, or maybe as street performers do, using volunteers to anchor and keep the audience.

The main reason not to use a volunteer is if you haven't thought through your technique and you are creating an enemy, not only of your volunteer but of your entire audience who identify with the person you choose.

When to choose a volunteer?

There are three 'when' to contemplate with regards to choosing volunteers: before the show, in the moment, or as part of your show.

Before the show is when most professional volunteer-users, like pickpockets or clowns with pure volunteer acts, would choose their volunteers. Mingling with the crowd before the show can give great insight as to your possible choices. Then you have to make sure you know exactly where they are sitting, and check they have not left for popcorn right before your act.

In the moment is probably the most used technique; it simply means that quickly and painlessly, without any pre-planning or forethought, performers scan the audience and pick who they feel is the best choice to bring on stage.

As part of the show is the same as 'in the moment' except that the artist chooses to use the audience's fear of being picked so the selection process becomes a drawn-out and uncomfortable routine in itself.

Who to choose as a volunteer?

- *Star of the day*

  The easiest person to choose as a volunteer is the star of the audience. The birthday celebrant, the going-away person, the boss. You know this person is right because they will get a bigger applause than you will. It is easiest because the audience and the star instinctively know they have the right to be on stage.

- *Status*

  Status is extremely important when choosing a volunteer. Making clear status choices increases comedy potential. If you are playfully abusive to someone higher status than yourself the audience will laugh (especially if you can get your volunteer to enjoy the game), but if you are playfully abusive to someone lower status than yourself the audience will immediately hate you. Whether the volunteer is lower or higher status in relation to the performer, changes the whole game. Different interactions based on status can totally change the face of the same routine.

- *Practical*

  There could be purely practical reasons for choosing volunteers, like needing five people to hold each side of a rope that you will balance on. In this case, the performer's needs would lead them to the simple choice of choosing strong people. Remember though that maybe ten kids on each side is a much stronger and potentially more hilarious routine than two strong men.

- *Body Language*

  This is the final way of choosing volunteers. My favourite volunteer is the person sending mixed body messages. They are partly saying they want to play but partly they are saying they are afraid or unsure. For instance, sometimes kids might have their hand up but are leaning backwards instead of forwards. Adults show they are keen by making eye contact and laughing slightly, but are still clearly nervous.

  Be extremely careful of volunteers who really want to come on stage. They usually have drives, needs and motivations other than actually wanting to play with you. In the end you really just want someone who will play with you, and not someone who will play with the audience without you.

Using Volunteers In Your Show

The basic rule of using volunteers it to make them feel smart and loved. Remember that each member of the audience sees themselves through the eyes of the volunteer. Yes you can get quick laughs by showing how confused and stupid they are, but then the audience will hate you as you obviously hate them.

Using volunteers shifts the focus of the game from the performer and the audience to a triangle between the performer, the volunteer and the audience. The most common mistake made by performers is to bring a volunteer on stage and then to forget about them due to only focusing on their own relationship with the audience. This kills the main reason for using volunteers. It is the actual connection and playfulness between the performer and the volunteer that becomes the new game.

To create this connection and playfulness we once again return to the basic skills of the performer. First, once the volunteer is chosen, you can play any game you want to get them on stage, but if they feel forced or uncomfortable you have already lost the connection and the playfulness will not arise. My only tip is to actually just connect with them. Find a small game they can accept, like holding onto an object. Then ask them to take the game to the next level but stay in their comfort zone. Maybe you ask them to stand and hold the object high up. Then when you finally ask them to come on stage, they have already forgotten why that would be a problem.

Remember to let the audience confirm they are happy with the choice of volunteer and encourage them to show it by applauding and cheering. Do this before the volunteer has realized what they have let themselves in for. This is one of the strongest tools of volunteer-choosing; it immediately cancels out the fear of standing in front of the group as the group has already demonstrated their approval of the volunteer.

Clarity versus Confusion

As the idea is to primarily create a connection and sense of playfulness, I strongly recommend that in the beginning of the volunteer routine, the performer is extremely exact and clear as to what they are asking the volunteer to do. The volunteer is feeling insecure and all they want to do is what is right. This is very important to realise. The less precise you are, the bigger the chance to confuse them too early. They will do what is 'right' as long as you keep on updating them as to what the new 'right' is.

If you use them for a magic trick for instance, bring the volunteer on stage and stand them exactly where they should be with their body turned in the correct direction, holding whatever you need to be held in the exact position. Then, when both of you are happy, they can get an applause as a recognition of their effort. Clarity helps to keep the routine and material clean.

At some point though, once the flow is there and the volunteer understands the rules and is playing with you, there is a lot of comedy potential in being unclear and confusing them. Then of course there's the pay-off of being clear again and seeing their faces light up because they understand again!

The Applause

Finally, after you have played with the volunteer, remember that they are the stars and not you. Ennoble your volunteer. The audience instinctively knows that you created the situation, but they should give the volunteer ALL the applause. The more the merrier. Everyone knows that they are actually applauding the performer as well.

VII
The Rebel Creator

'There are no bad audiences.'

Nalleslavski

Being a rebel is built into the clown. Tell a group of clowns to go one way and no doubt they'll go the other. They'll swim through disorderly, nonsensical chaos to that place which, in the end, simply reflects the real pleasures and pains of being human. Turning the world upside down has never been so fun.

I believe the power of the performer is stronger than we give it credit for and performers have the responsibility of using their art to affect their community. Sometimes the community's sole desire may be a basic human need to be entertained. By 'entertainment' I don't mean TV which offers a fake sense of community. I mean the experience of a group of people seeing a live show together which gives them a real sense of kinship – a true sense of 'belonging' for that moment to the group of people who are having that experience together.

This is especially true for people who have experienced trauma, and it's important as a performer to offer an experience which is something other than the current difficult situation in which these people find themselves. When we go on a Clowns Without Borders tour, we encourage the children to perceive the world with new eyes. We want to show them there are other possibilities besides the reality they're presently in.

Having Syrian refugees laugh at me at the Za'atari camp in the north of Jordan doesn't feel that different to being laughed at in a burlesque strip club in Stockholm. In both instances it's a large group of people who are somehow in that moment losing their individuality to a group. They become a collective audience laughing at the same time at whatever it is you're doing on stage, and you are controlling that laughter. There's a feeling of magic when that happens. It's what I mean when I say 'the room turns red'.

My art is the art of affecting the audience. It doesn't have to be about laughter, it's never only been about that, it's about giving the audience an emotional experience. I'm not really interested in the innate talent of the performer or even the art form they choose to channel their talent through. What is most important to me is the fine connection to the audience, the basic meeting. Once performers understand they can mould how the audience will react, their own political agendas can begin to inform their choices.

What we need for audiences in this day and age is nothing less than rebel creators, performers who take the development of their craft and ability into their own hands, creating a sense of connection and playfulness with whatever audience they happen to find themselves in front of.

In this book I've shared bits of my accumulated knowledge, fragments of my learning and teaching from over fifteen years in the performance field. I urge you to take them or leave them in whichever way you wish, but my suggestion is to remember that whatever happens and whatever your choices, happiness is most important. Easy.

Photograph © Tomas Blideman

WWW.OBERONBOOKS.COM